REFLECTIONS
FOR
LENT

13 February – 30 March 2013

STEPHEN COTTRELL
STEVEN CROFT
BARBARA MOSSE
MARK OAKLEY

with an introduction by
JANE WILLIAMS

Church House Publishing
Church House
Great Smith Street
London SW1P 3AZ

ISBN 978 0 7151 4306 3

Published 2012 by Church House Publishing
Copyright © The Archbishops' Council 2012

The opinions expressed in this book are those of the
authors and do not necessarily reflect the official policy of
the General Synod or The Archbishops' Council of the
Church of England.

Designed and typeset by Hugh Hillyard-Parker
Printed and bound by CPI Group (UK) Ltd, Croydon, CR0 4YY

Contents

About the authors

Stephen Cottrell is the Bishop of Chelmsford. Before this he was bishop of Reading and has worked in parishes in London, Chichester, and Huddersfield and as Pastor of Peterborough Cathedral. He is a well-known writer and speaker on evangelism, spirituality and catechesis. His best selling *How to Pray* (CHP) and *How to Live* (CHP) have recently been re-issued.

Steven Croft is the Bishop of Sheffield. He was previously Warden of Cranmer Hall, and team leader of Fresh Expressions. He is the author of a number of books including *Jesus People: what next for the church?* and *The Advent Calendar*, a novel for children and adults.

Barbara Mosse is an Anglican priest and writer, and since 2006 has been Lecturer in Christian Spirituality at Sarum College, Salisbury. Alongside parish work, she has varied chaplaincy experience in prison, university, community mental health and hospital. Her book *The Treasures of Darkness* was published by Canterbury Press in 2003.

Mark Oakley is Canon Treasurer of St Paul's Cathedral. A former Chaplain to the Bishop of London and Rector of St Paul's, Covent Garden, he is also the author of *The Collage of God* (2001) and various anthologies, articles and reviews, usually in the areas of faith, poetry and literature.

John Pritchard is the Bishop of Oxford. Prior to that he has been Bishop of Jarrow, Archdeacon of Canterbury and Warden of Cranmer Hall, Durham. His only ambition was to be a vicar, which he was in Taunton for eight happy years. He enjoys armchair sport, walking, reading, music, theatre and recovering.

Jane Williams lectures at St Mellitus College, London and Chelmsford, and is a visiting lecturer at King's College London. She taught previously at Trinity Theological College, Bristol.

About *Reflections for Daily Prayer*

Based on the *Common Worship Lectionary* readings for Morning Prayer, these daily reflections are designed to refresh and inspire times of personal prayer. The aim is to provide rich, contemporary and engaging insights into Scripture.

Each page lists the lectionary readings for the day, with the main psalms for that day highlighted in **bold**. The Collect of the day – either the *Common Worship* collect or the shorter additional collect – is also included.

For those using this book in conjunction with a service of Morning Prayer, the following conventions apply: a psalm printed in parentheses is omitted if it has been used as the opening canticle at that office; a psalm marked with an asterisk may be shortened if desired.

A short reflection is provided on either the Old or New Testament reading. Popular writers, experienced ministers, biblical scholars and theologians will be contributing to this series. They all bring their own emphases, enthusiasms and approaches to biblical interpretation to bear.

Regular users of Morning Prayer and *Time to Pray* (from *Common Worship: Daily Prayer*) and anyone who follows the lectionary for their regular Bible reading will benefit from the rich variety of traditions represented in these stimulating and accessible pieces.

What is Lent for?

Lent is a time for rediscovering our freedom and remembering that we are new creatures in a new world.

It may seem odd that we do this by 'giving things up', or exercising discipline, but that is because we find it so hard to believe that we are indeed free and so hard to live in that freedom. When Moses led the Israelites out of slavery in Egypt, they were not grateful for long before they started to yearn for their old captivity. They remembered the security of being slaves, the fact that they never had to take decisions about their own lives, or worry about where the next meal was coming from (see Exodus 16.3). They looked back with nostalgia to the time when they lived like animals, rather than human beings, conveniently forgetting that animals may be abused or petted, but they are not free.

In our case, our freedom is usually more insidiously undermined. We forget that the things that we can't manage without, the things we depend on, the things that define us, also master us. So for the 40 days of Lent, we work our way back to essentials, to find out again who we are.

Our quest starts with Jesus as our model. Jesus is told, unequivocally, by a voice from heaven, just who he is: the beloved Son of God. In our baptism, that is what we are all told, and that becomes our defining theme. But, strangely, Jesus then retreats to the desert, far away from all other voices, to hear the echo of the Father's voice and trace its effect on his life.

In the desert, Jesus trains himself to understand his true nature and his real freedom: the freedom to do God's will and to be God's child, under all circumstances. In order to find that reality, he rejects three iconic illusions of human freedom. He rejects the temptation to turn stones into bread, which is the temptation to material security, to 'storing up treasure on earth'. We all long to know that we will always have enough, but that harmless longing can so easily become the one thing that we live for.

Next, Jesus rejects the temptation to power. He is offered 'all the kingdoms of the world', and rejects them, not because power is always a bad thing, but because he sees with painful clarity where this power comes from and where it must lead. Jesus exercised power during his earthly life and continues to exercise it at the right hand of the Father, who is the only source of life-giving power. All other kinds lead only to death.

And finally, Jesus rejects the temptation to selfish, possessive love. He is asked to put God's love to the test, and to prove to himself that he is the favourite, but he refuses. His life will prove that God's beloved children demonstrate God's favour by sharing it.

These hard choices in the wilderness win Jesus his freedom: he is free to be who and what he is, under all circumstances; nothing can make him untrue to himself and his calling, and nothing can hold him captive, not even death.

Every Lent, we get the chance to set ourselves free again by asking ourselves those questions. Has our search for material security come to dominate our lives? Are we exercising the power we have under the authority of God, and to help others to flourish? Have our relationships become self-centred and ungenerous? This is a good time to make space in our lives to hear again the defining voice of God, calling us his beloved children, and to let that voice set us free.

Most of our little habits are not wicked, but the problem is that they can still be enslaving: they tell us what we must do and have and be, and they muffle out the voice of God. So now we have 40 days to look truthfully at what enslaves us, and to begin to exercise our freedom. That might mean eating less, or spending less, or giving things and money away, because we do not live by bread alone. It might mean re-thinking how we treat work colleagues, or strangers at the bus stop or on the road or in the supermarket, because the kingdoms of this earth are God's not ours. Or it might mean spending more time with friends and family, putting their needs above ours, because we do not need to be at the centre of the world to know we are beloved.

Here are 40 days to exercise our freedom to be only who and what we are in God's eyes, and to remind ourselves that, in God's redeemed world, nothing more is necessary.

Jane Williams

The importance of daily prayer

Daily prayer is a way of sustaining that most special of all relationships. It helps if we want to pray, but it can be sufficient to want to want to pray, or even to want to want to want to pray! The direction of the heart is what matters, not its achievements. Gradually we are shaped and changed by the practice of daily prayer. Apprentices in prayer never graduate, but we become a little bit more the people God wants us to be.

Prayer isn't a technique; it's a relationship, and it starts in the most ordinary, instinctive reactions to everyday life:

- **Gratitude**: good things are always happening to us, however small.
- **Wonder**: we often see amazing things in nature and in people but pass them by.
- **Need**: we bump into scores of needs every day.
- **Sorrow**: we mess up.

Prayer is taking those instincts and stretching them out before God. The rules then are: start small, stay natural, be honest.

Here are four ways of putting some structure around daily prayer.

1 The Quiet Time. This is the classic way of reading a passage of the Bible, using Bible reading reflections like those in this book, and then praying naturally about the way the passage has struck you, taking to God the questions, resolutions, hopes, fears and other responses that have arisen within you.

2 The Daily Office. This is a structured way of reading scripture and psalms, and praying for individuals, the world, the day ahead, etc. It keeps us anchored in the Lectionary, the basic reading of the Church, and so ensures that we engage with the breadth of scripture, rather than just with our favourite passages. It also puts us in living touch with countless others around the world who are doing something similar. A simple form can be found on the inside front and back covers of this book. Fuller forms can be found in *Common Worship: Daily Prayer*.

3 **Holy Reading**. Also known as *Lectio Divina*, this is a tried and trusted way of feeding and meditating on the Bible, described more fully on pages 4–5 of this book. In essence, here is how it is done:

- *Read:* Read the passage slowly until a phrase catches your attention.
- *Reflect:* Chew the phrase carefully, drawing the goodness out of it.
- *Respond:* Pray about the thoughts and feelings that have surfaced in you.
- *Rest:* You may want to rest in silence for a while.
- *Repeat:* Carry on with the passage …

4 **Silence**. In our distracted culture some people are drawn more to silence than to words. This will involve *centring* (hunkering down), *focusing* on a short biblical phrase (e.g. 'Come, Holy Spirit'), *waiting* (repeating the phrase as necessary), and *ending* (perhaps with the Lord's Prayer). The length of time is irrelevant.

There are, of course, as many ways of praying as there are people to pray. There are no right or wrong ways to pray. 'Pray as you can, not as you can't', is wise advice. The most important thing is to make sure there is sufficient structure to keep prayer going when it's a struggle as well as when it's a joy. Prayer is too important to leave to chance.

+John Pritchard

Lectio Divina – a way of reading the Bible

Lectio Divina is a contemplative way of reading the Bible. It dates back to the early centuries of the Christian Church and was established as a monastic practice by Benedict in the 6th century. It is a way of praying the scriptures that leads us deeper into God's word. We slow down. We read a short passage more than once. We chew it over slowly and carefully. We savour it. Scripture begins to speak to us in a new way. It speaks to us personally, and aids that union we have with God through Christ who is himself the Living Word.

Make sure you are sitting comfortably. Breathe slowly and deeply. Ask God to speak to you through the passage that you are about to read.

This way of praying starts with our silence. We often make the mistake of thinking prayer is about what we say to God. It is actually the other way round. God wants to speak to us. He will do this through the scriptures. So don't worry about what to say. Don't worry if nothing jumps out at you at first. God is patient. He will wait for the opportunity to get in. He will give you a word and lead you to understand its meaning for you today.

First reading: Listen

As you read the passage listen for a word or phrase that attracts you. Allow it to arise from the passage as if it is God's word for you today. Sit in silence repeating the word or phrase in your head.

Then say the word or phrase aloud.

Second reading: Ponder

As you read the passage again, ask how this word or phrase speaks to your life and why it has connected with you. Ponder it carefully. Don't worry if you get distracted – it may be part of your response to offer to God. Sit in silence and then frame a single sentence that begins to say aloud what this word or phrase says to you.

Third reading: Pray

As you read the passage for the last time, ask what Christ is calling from you. What is it that you need to do or consider or relinquish or take on as a result of what God is saying to you in this word or phrase? In the silence that follows the reading, pray for the grace of the Spirit to plant this word in your heart.

If you are in a group, talk for a few minutes and pray with each other.

If you are on your own, speak your prayer to God either aloud or in the silence of your heart.

If there is time, you may even want to read the passage a fourth time, and then end with the same silence before God with which you began.

+Stephen Cottrell

Wednesday 13 February

Ash Wednesday

Psalm **38**
Daniel 9.3-6, 17-19
1 Timothy 6.6-19

1 Timothy 6.6-19

*'Of course, there is great gain in godliness combined
with contentment' (v.6)*

Today marks the beginning of the season of Lent, and with it, childhood memories of the yearly urging to 'give up' something for the season. What was given up was not that important, although apparently it only 'worked' if it was something I really liked. It became a matter of some pride to see if I could hold out until Easter Sunday, when I could thankfully relax and gorge on all the chocolate I had self-righteously denied myself.

Time thankfully brought a bit more wisdom to the process, and with it the realization that Lent offers a precious opportunity to reflect on our attitude to 'things' – both those we have, and those we lack. Here, Paul is warning Timothy to beware of greed in all its forms: the greed that manifests itself as a 'morbid craving' for controversy (v.4), or as a love of money which is 'a root of all kinds of evil' (v.10). Even the pursuit of godliness can become a twisted form of greed (v.5). The way forward, says Paul, is to pursue godliness *with contentment* (v.6), a quality conspicuously missing from our grasping human behaviour.

How content are we with what we have? Whether or not we choose to give something up, this season offers us an opportunity – with the guidance of the Holy Spirit – to examine our own tendency to greed and acquisitiveness, and to seek God's healing and transformation.

COLLECT

Almighty and everlasting God,
you hate nothing that you have made
and forgive the sins of all those who are penitent:
create and make in us new and contrite hearts
that we, worthily lamenting our sins
and acknowledging our wretchedness,
may receive from you, the God of all mercy,
perfect remission and forgiveness;
through Jesus Christ your Son our Lord,
who is alive and reigns with you,
in the unity of the Holy Spirit,
one God, now and for ever.

Psalms **77** *or* **37***
Jeremiah 2.14-32
John 4.1-26

John 4.1-26

'Sir, give me this water, so that I may never be thirsty …' (v.15)

With Jesus, things are never predictable. In our very different time and context, over-familiarity with this incident may well blind us to its original shock value. Jesus openly challenges and breaks through two boundaries: that between the chosen people (the Jews) and those rejected (the Samaritans), and between male and female. The woman herself is taken aback by Jesus' request, recognizing his breach of both boundaries: 'How is it that you, a Jew, ask a drink of me, a woman of Samaria?' (v.9). In his approach to the woman, Jesus challenges each one of us in our natural human tendency to assess others, on whatever grounds – race, gender, age, religion, sexual orientation – in terms of inclusion or exclusion. He is inviting those who claim to be disciples to join him in breaking through those boundaries, instead of helping to construct them and keep them in place.

But the challenge goes deeper than this. Jesus offers living water, and the woman's immediate response is to rejoice at the idea of a permanent quenching of physical thirst and the redundancy of a boring and repetitive chore (vv.13-15). So often we approach God on the basis of our immediate perceived need, and indeed, Christ himself urges us to do this (Matthew 7 7-11). But he also beckons us deeper – beyond our surface desires to that fountain of living water that alone can sustain and nurture us for all eternity.

Holy God,
our lives are laid open before you:
rescue us from the chaos of sin
and through the death of your Son
bring us healing and make us whole
in Jesus Christ our Lord.

COLLECT

Friday 15 February

John 4.27-42

'My food is to do the will of him who sent me ...' (v.34)

When we attempt to make sense of our world, we tend in the first instance to default to a literalistic interpretation. This was certainly true with the Samaritan woman in her initial reaction to Jesus' offer of living water (v.15), and we saw yesterday how Jesus took the time and patience to lead her gently from a literal to a much deeper understanding of his words (v.14).

But it was not only the woman who needed this form of teaching. As she returns to the city to tell others about Jesus, the disciples rejoin him and urge him to have something to eat. Jesus' enigmatic reply – 'I have food to eat that you do not know about (v.32) – has the disciples wondering who else could have brought him some food (v.33). But they, like the woman, need to be drawn into a deeper understanding (v.34).

As Jesus addresses his original hearers, so he also addresses us. He urges us to move beyond what we know and to be dissatisfied with a merely superficial interpretation of our experience. The divine reality shimmers beneath the surface of the mundane and the everyday, and Jesus challenges us to deepen our vision so that we may see the gifts that he offers us *now*, in the present moment, whatever its complexities and ambiguities. Now as then, Jesus takes familiar images and charges them with new life and meaning.

COLLECT

Almighty and everlasting God,
you hate nothing that you have made
and forgive the sins of all those who are penitent:
create and make in us new and contrite hearts
that we, worthily lamenting our sins
and acknowledging our wretchedness,
may receive from you, the God of all mercy,
perfect remission and forgiveness;
through Jesus Christ your Son our Lord,
who is alive and reigns with you,
in the unity of the Holy Spirit,
one God, now and for ever.

John 4.43-end

'Unless you see signs and wonders you will not believe' (v.48)

The scene has changed, but the teaching remains consistent. Jesus moves on to Galilee, and is welcomed by everyone 'since they had seen all that he had done in Jerusalem at the festival' (v.45). People again are drawn because of the signs he has done, and the Gospel writer locates Jesus very precisely, at the place of his first 'sign': 'at Cana … where he had changed the water into wine' (v.46).

And here, a royal official requests another sign: that Jesus will come and heal his dying son (v.47). There is no indication that he has previously known Jesus, but he has clearly heard of Jesus' reputation and his own need is desperate. Jesus' initial response is not encouraging (v.48), but the official is not deterred; he trusts to Jesus' compassion and holds firm to his purpose.

The official's son is healed – but we know that our prayers for healing are not always answered in the way we might have wished. But just as the official received more than he realized he needed – the gift of faith – so too we are encouraged to approach Christ in faith and trust, open to the depths and the mystery of the work he longs to do in us. It is right that we bring our requests to God, but his loving response to the needs of our aching hearts will always be deeper than we can consciously grasp or imagine.

Holy God,
our lives are laid open before you:
rescue us from the chaos of sin
and through the death of your Son
bring us healing and make us whole
in Jesus Christ our Lord.

COLLECT

Psalms 10, 11 *or* 44
Jeremiah 4.19-end
John 5.1-18

John 5.1-18

'Do you want to be made well?' (v.6)

What an astonishing question for Jesus to ask a sick man! Ill for 38 years, the anonymous invalid by the pool of Beth-zatha had always been beaten in the rush to enter the waters by his more able-bodied peers. So he must have been desperate to be made well – mustn't he?

But Jesus again demonstrates his instinctive awareness of the tendencies of human nature. Why did he address *this* man, rather than the others? It was because he 'saw him lying there and knew that he had been there a long time' (v.6). We sometimes hear of people who have 'enjoyed bad health for many years'. Enjoyed what? Not the pain and inconvenience, obviously – but what about all the extra attention and freedom from responsibility illness temporarily brings? In such cases, it may take courage to seize the opportunity for health should it be offered. Such a prospect could be daunting, and may encourage the chronic sufferer to use their sickness as a protective shield.

So Jesus asks the man, do you *want* to be made well? Satisfied with the man's response, he tells him bluntly, 'Stand up, take your mat and walk' (v.8). Chronic illness is a complex issue, and not all situations will be amenable to the urging to, quite literally, 'stand on your own feet'. But this passage does perhaps encourage us to risk asking Jesus' question of ourselves: do we *want* to be made well?

COLLECT

Almighty God,
whose Son Jesus Christ fasted forty days in the wilderness,
and was tempted as we are, yet without sin:
give us grace to discipline ourselves in obedience to your Spirit;
and, as you know our weakness,
so may we know your power to save;
through Jesus Christ your Son our Lord,
who is alive and reigns with you,
in the unity of the Holy Spirit,
one God, now and for ever.

Psalms **44** *or* **48,** 52
Jeremiah 5.1-19
John 5.19-29

John 5.19-29

'… the Son can do nothing on his own' (v.19)

At the end of yesterday's reading the Jews start persecuting Jesus (v.16), not only because he was healing on the Sabbath, but also because his claim that God was his Father suggested equality with him (v.18). Jesus' response to their accusations demonstrates how totally dependent he is on his Father: 'the Son can do nothing on his own, but only what he sees the Father doing' (v.19).

In the Christian life, it is not always easy to find a healthy balance between self-reliance and dependency. In yesterday's reading, Jesus healed a man who had been sick for 38 years. At Jesus' word, the man found the inner courage and trust to get to his feet; he had his part to play, without which there would have been no healing. The words 'step out in faith' when applied to our journey are often quite literally intended.

But if even Jesus was unable to act independently of his Father, how much more must that be true of us! Our own strength is insufficient; the close relationship Jesus reports requires a constant, concentrated looking towards God, listening for the murmur of his word in the silent depths of our heart. This reality echoes down to us from scripture and through the writings of all those who through the centuries have sought a closer walk with God: 'For God alone my soul waits in silence; from him comes my salvation' (Psalm 62.1).

COLLECT

Heavenly Father,
your Son battled with the powers of darkness,
and grew closer to you in the desert:
help us to use these days to grow in wisdom and prayer
that we may witness to your saving love
in Jesus Christ our Lord.

Psalms **6**, 17 *or* **119.57-80**
Jeremiah 5.20-end
John 5.30-end

John 5.30-end

'As I hear, I judge; and my judgement is just …' (v.30)

The question of judging is something of a vexed one in the New Testament. Is it not a good thing to use our judgement to distinguish right from wrong? And yet in Luke's Gospel, Jesus urges his hearers to neither judge nor condemn (Luke 6.37); and Paul in his letter to the Romans is equally trenchant: 'Therefore you have no excuse … when you judge others; for in passing judgement on another you condemn yourself, because you … are doing the very same things' (Romans 2.1).

Paul clearly pinpoints the problem when he states that, when we judge and condemn others, we so often fail to recognize the existence of the same faults within ourselves. We are experts at identifying the speck in our neighbour's eye, while failing to notice the log in our own (Luke 6.41).

In today's reading Jesus speaks of his own judgement, and his words indicate a reason for our own frequent failures. His dependency upon his Father is the key (v.30*a*), and he claims that his seeking of his Father's will in preference to his own is the foundation on which his correct judgement is made (v.30*b*).

In this life we can never be completely free from the influence of unconscious fears and motivations. But as we seek a closer relationship with God, our vision will be deepened and clarified, and we will increasingly be enabled to see the world through his eyes, rather than our own.

COLLECT

Almighty God,
whose Son Jesus Christ fasted forty days in the wilderness,
and was tempted as we are, yet without sin:
give us grace to discipline ourselves in obedience to your Spirit;
and, as you know our weakness,
so may we know your power to save;
through Jesus Christ your Son our Lord,
who is alive and reigns with you,
in the unity of the Holy Spirit,
one God, now and for ever.

Psalms **42**, 43 *or* 56, **57** (63*)
Jeremiah 6.9-21
John 6.1-15

John 6.1-15

'Jesus ... withdrew again to the mountain by himself' (v.15)

Jesus is persistently misunderstood by the crowds who flock to him. Today's passage opens with a large crowd following him 'because they saw the signs he was doing for the sick' (v.2). He satisfies their physical hunger through a feeding miracle, and the pressure intensifies as they then hail him as a prophet (v.14) and desire to make him king (v.15). This leaves Jesus little option but to withdraw to protect his true identity, because that identity can never be confined within human categories of power and authority, nor be twisted to serve a merely human self-interest.

But this withdrawal may signify more than simply a desire to disabuse the crowd of their wrong thinking. The graphic accounts of Jesus' time in the wilderness in Matthew (4.1-11) and Luke (4.1-12) make it vividly clear that the temptation to take the way of worldly power and acclaim was *real*. In recent days we have been reflecting on Jesus' total dependence on his Father and his inability to act rightly independently of that relationship. So this withdrawal enables Jesus to resist again the lure of earthly power and to strengthen his prayerful dependence on his Father (see Luke 5.16; Matthew 14.23).

When our actions bring praise and admiration, it can be difficult to resist the flattering ego-boost such praise generates. At such times an inner 'withdrawal' may help to remind us where the source of our abilities truly lies.

Heavenly Father,
your Son battled with the powers of darkness,
and grew closer to you in the desert:
help us to use these days to grow in wisdom and prayer
that we may witness to your saving love
in Jesus Christ our Lord.

COLLECT

15

John 6.16-27

'It is I; do not be afraid' (v.20)

The storm on the lake that follows Jesus' withdrawal to the mountain is reminiscent of another episode where Jesus calmed both a storm and his disciples' fear of drowning (Mark 4.35-41). But there are significant differences. In the Markan episode, Jesus accompanied the disciples in the boat and calmed the storm, chiding them for their lack of faith. In today's passage, the disciples' fear is of Jesus, and it is *that* fear that Jesus addresses, rather than the turbulence of the wind and waves.

But Jesus' words hold a deeper significance, one veiled in our English translations. In the original Greek these words read 'I AM (*ego eimi*); do not be afraid.' To disciples steeped in the holy scriptures, such words would have had deep resonance: the God who had first revealed himself as 'I AM', the shield and protector of Abram (Genesis 15.1), and to Moses by the same name in the burning bush (Exodus 3.1-6), was now revealing himself afresh to them in the person of Jesus Christ.

Jesus here reveals his glory and his true identity, not in order to amaze the crowds, but to calm the fear of his terrified disciples. With them we are invited to ponder the awe-inspiring mystery of I AM, and to respond with gratitude to the gift of God in Christ. He is ever-living, ever-present, and approaches us through all the storms of life, breathing his peace into our deepest fears.

COLLECT

Almighty God,
whose Son Jesus Christ fasted forty days in the wilderness,
and was tempted as we are, yet without sin:
give us grace to discipline ourselves in obedience to your Spirit;
and, as you know our weakness,
so may we know your power to save;
through Jesus Christ your Son our Lord,
who is alive and reigns with you,
in the unity of the Holy Spirit,
one God, now and for ever.

Psalms 59, **63** *or* **68**
Jeremiah 7.1-20
John 6.27-40

John 6.27-40

'Do not work for the food that perishes ...' (v.27)

The storm-interlude over, Jesus is again surrounded by the crowds. Their persistent pursuit (vv.22-26) feels like harassment, and Jesus confronts them bluntly with their real motivation: that he had earlier satisfied their physical hunger and they want him to do so again (v.26). But the kind of food they are seeking will never adequately satisfy; its effects are temporary and it will ultimately perish (v.27). The dialogue between Jesus and the crowd here has much in common with his earlier conversation with the Samaritan woman at the well. In both, the first instinct is the desire for physical sustenance; Jesus then uses that desire to point the seeker(s) beyond their physical need to the nourishment that is eternal (true bread/living water), and finally to himself as the true source of that nourishment (6.35; 4.14).

Through his patient teaching and leading of the crowd, Jesus challenges their and our stubborn human capacity for only seeing what is immediately in front of our noses. The crowd wants to stick with the security of Moses; where are our sticking points? When is it that we say to God, 'this far and no further'? 'Whoever comes to me will never be hungry, and whoever believes in me will never be thirsty' (v.35). Jesus' glorious promise inevitably challenges our tendency to cling on to what we think we know, rather than risk stepping into the unknown with Christ as our guide.

Heavenly Father,
your Son battled with the powers of darkness,
and grew closer to you in the desert:
help us to use these days to grow in wisdom and prayer
that we may witness to your saving love
in Jesus Christ our Lord.

COLLECT

Monday 25 February

Psalms 26, **32** *or* **71**
Jeremiah 7.21-end
John 6.41-51

John 6.41-51

'I am the bread of life' (v.48)

This reading makes things clear. Like bread, Jesus is the most basic thing we need. So having been fed so abundantly with the sliced white variety one day, the crowds come back to Jesus the next day, hungry for more. Of course they do! Who wouldn't! And, of course, they expect he will have something to say to them. They're not stupid. There was bound to be some moral string attached somewhere. Even in those days they reckoned that there wasn't really such thing as a free lunch. Now they would find out. But they thought Jesus was going to tell them to behave themselves, to be nice to each other. What they didn't expect to hear was this: he *is* the lunch. The food they had yesterday was a signpost to the real bread, which is him. More than this, he is saying that this is the bread they really crave. Like manna – bread from heaven – Jesus is himself the basic survival rations of the desert. The bread they got yesterday will fill them for a day, and then they will need more. But if they eat *this* bread, they will live forever. There is a free lunch after all. It is on offer here, but accepting it is mighty hard.

One by one they complain. Their sneers are predictable. Isn't this Jesus? Joseph's boy? Where does he get this nonsense?

COLLECT

Almighty God,
you show to those who are in error the light of your truth,
that they may return to the way of righteousness:
grant to all those who are admitted
    into the fellowship of Christ's religion,
that they may reject those things
    that are contrary to their profession,
and follow all such things as are agreeable to the same;
through our Lord Jesus Christ,
who is alive and reigns with you,
in the unity of the Holy Spirit,
one God, now and for ever.

Psalms **50** *or* **73**
Jeremiah 8.1-15
John 6.52-59

John 6.52-59

'… my flesh is true food and my blood is true drink' (v.55)

The complaints turn to disputes, 'How can this man give us his flesh to eat?' These are people who want their religion credible and fair. God up in heaven and them down below. Good deeds rewarded. Sinners condemned.

Jesus challenges all of it. Everyone is fed: the deserving and the undeserving sharing the same ever-expanding table. No one left out. This is bad enough, but since the meal itself is the flesh of the Son of Man – Jesus' flesh, true food; his blood, true drink – it is not a message (or a meal!) that anyone can stomach.

It is incredible: eternal life offered through this Nazarene, Jesus, Joseph's son, claiming to be the bread from heaven. And it is unfair, a rather too liberal banquet where anyone who turns up is welcomed in, where there is no differentiation. After all, isn't differentiation what it's all about? A particular people with a particular God and a particular law. That is how God abides in you. All this 'bread from heaven' stuff is seriously undermining. Little wonder that people walk away.

Though as we watch them it might be worth considering what it is about the generosity of God, as it is shown us in Jesus, that we find so offensive. In a Church that is sadly not without its disputes, we might do well to ask ourselves this.

Almighty God,
by the prayer and discipline of Lent
may we enter into the mystery of Christ's sufferings,
and by following in his Way
come to share in his glory;
through Jesus Christ our Lord.

COLLECT

19

Lent

Wednesday 27 February

Psalms **35** *or* **77**
Jeremiah 8.18 – 9.11
John 6.60-end

John 6.60-end

'Lord, to whom can we go?' (v.68)

Even the disciples are pushed to the limits. Who can accept this difficult teaching? And for some of them it is too much. Like the dispersing crowds, they leave Jesus. And then we come to one of the saddest and most beautiful exchanges in all of scripture. Alone with the Twelve, Jesus asks them, 'Do you wish to go away as well?' Simon Peter answers: 'Lord to whom we can go?' And first of all we should perhaps acknowledge that these are not necessarily words of great faithfulness. It could be that Peter is saying, 'Yes. I would love to go. Please show me the exit'. But he continues: 'We have come to believe and know that you are the Holy One of God' (v.69). In other words, there isn't anywhere else to go. Once you have seen that Jesus of Nazareth is the Holy One of God, then however difficult, however challenging, however uncomfortable it is, there is no turning back.

Peter is caught in the snare of God's purposes and his love for us in Jesus Christ. He can't understand it, or work it out, but he knows that there is nothing else. And you could also say that Judas' betrayal is rooted in his own inability to accept Jesus as food and drink. He wants an explanation, not a gospel.

COLLECT

Almighty God,
you show to those who are in error the light of your truth,
that they may return to the way of righteousness:
grant to all those who are admitted
    into the fellowship of Christ's religion,
that they may reject those things
    that are contrary to their profession,
and follow all such things as are agreeable to the same;
through our Lord Jesus Christ,
who is alive and reigns with you,
in the unity of the Holy Spirit,
one God, now and for ever.

Psalms **34** *or* **78.1-39***
Jeremiah 9.12-24
John 7.1-13

John 7.1-13

'My time has not yet come' (v.6)

'No one who wants to be widely known acts in secret' (v.4). What could be more obvious? If, on the one hand, you have made who you are so plain, why, on the other hand, hide away in Galilee. Go to Judea. Go to the festival. Make yourself known. This is Jesus' dilemma, and also a dilemma for those who follow him. Is it fear? The Jewish authorities are certainly beginning to conspire against him. Well, that's what it looks like. But for Jesus it is something else. It is timing. What Jesus is going to reveal is a leadership and a purpose that will be very different from what everyone is imagining, even those who have now recognized who he is, the Holy One of God. For he is not just living bread, but also wine poured out. There will be a time for this sort of leadership to be revealed. Later on, Jesus will say that it is only when he is lifted up that people will really understand who he is (see John 8.28). It is only when he is lifted onto the cross that the timing will be right.

Part of our Lenten discipline is to see Jesus as he really is, and that can also only happen on the cross. And then to see him as living bread and wine poured out, the most basic thing we need.

Almighty God,
by the prayer and discipline of Lent
may we enter into the mystery of Christ's sufferings,
and by following in his Way
come to share in his glory;
through Jesus Christ our Lord.

COLLECT

Friday 1 March

John 7.14-24

'My teaching is not mine but his who sent me' (v.16)

Now Jesus is at the festival after all. No longer hidden away, he teaches openly. And the Jews are astonished by what he says. 'How does this man have such learning, when he has never been taught himself?' (v.15) On the one hand, they are genuinely amazed; on the other, it is something of a put down, a familiar jibe levelled against those who don't necessarily have the right qualifications, or who didn't attend the right schools. Jesus' response is swift and damning. His teaching is not his own, but from God. His learning flows from his relationship with the one he calls Father. This is not the second-hand knowledge that the bright can easily acquire, not something captured in a book or downloaded to your phone, but something that only comes from the relationship with God that he is offering.

And the sting in the tail, just as sharp for us today as it was to those who listened to Jesus then: if you had truly resolved to do God's will, to dwell in this relationship and to see in Jesus God's abiding presence, then you wouldn't ask the question in the first place. You would know that the teaching is from God. Now there's something to think about as we examine our own discipleship. Are we that close to God?

COLLECT

Almighty God,
you show to those who are in error the light of your truth,
that they may return to the way of righteousness:
grant to all those who are admitted
    into the fellowship of Christ's religion,
that they may reject those things
    that are contrary to their profession,
and follow all such things as are agreeable to the same;
through our Lord Jesus Christ,
who is alive and reigns with you,
in the unity of the Holy Spirit,
one God, now and for ever.

Psalms 3, **25** *or* **76**, 79
Jeremiah 10.17-24
John 7.25-36

John 7.25-36

'I know him, because I am from him, and he sent me' (v.29)

More confusion. And it is all about identity. The religious authorities said they were going to kill Jesus, but now they look on impassively while he speaks so openly. Perhaps they actually know that he is who he claims to be, the Messiah from God? But this can't be so, because they all know where this Jesus comes from, and also know that when the Messiah comes, no one will know where he's from. Meanwhile Jesus insists that they may know his address on earth, but it is his dwelling place with God that really matters. That's where he's come from.

This is the claim Jesus keeps coming back to. It is the root of his identity and his mission. Even more confusing, he says 'I have not come on my own' (v.28). These words foreshadow Jesus' words to Philip: 'Whoever has seen me has seen the Father' (John 14.9). God has *sent* Jesus and is at the same time *with* Jesus. In Jesus, there is this continuity and community between the Son and the Father. It is what we Christians have come to understand as Trinity. 'I know him because I am from him. He has sent me,' says Jesus. God is present with him in his every word and deed. And as he makes this clear, they again try to arrest him. But it still isn't the time, and Jesus evades them.

Almighty God,
by the prayer and discipline of Lent
may we enter into the mystery of Christ's sufferings,
and by following in his Way
come to share in his glory;
through Jesus Christ our Lord.

COLLECT

23

Monday 4 March

Psalms **5**, 7 *or* **80**, 82
Jeremiah 11.1-17
John 7.37-52

John 7.37-52

'Let anyone who is thirsty come to me' (v.37)

I can only remember one occasion in my life when I've been really thirsty. Even that was only for a few hours, but when I was able to slake my aching thirst, it was a fantastic relief. My whole being was irrigated and refreshed. Well, if you've ever been just a little bit thirsty, and known that longing for cool, fresh water, then you'll have an inkling of the power of these words. Jesus offers himself as one who can quench thirst: 'If you believe in me,' says Jesus, 'drink.' It is an astonishing invitation.

But it goes further. Alluding to the Holy Spirit, Jesus says that if we drink from him, then gushing streams of living water will not just flow into our lives, they will flow out of them as well. We too will become a source of blessing. Jesus will give himself to others through his giving of himself to us.

Everyone then carries on arguing about whether he is the Messiah or not, and stressing about the fact that he wasn't born in the right place. After all, Messiahs are supposed to have the right postcode. But Jesus has not just moved the goalposts, he has redrawn the whole map. He is now speaking and acting as if he is God's Messiah, and offering gifts that only God can give.

COLLECT

Almighty God,
whose most dear Son went not up to joy
    but first he suffered pain,
and entered not into glory before he was crucified:
mercifully grant that we, walking in the way of the cross,
may find it none other than the way of life and peace;
through Jesus Christ your Son our Lord,
who is alive and reigns with you,
in the unity of the Holy Spirit,
one God, now and for ever.

Psalms 6, **9** *or* 87, **89.1-18**
Jeremiah 11.18 – 12.6
John 7.53 – 8.11

John 7.53 – 8.11

*'Let anyone among you who is without sin be the first
to throw a stone at her' (8.7)*

'Teacher, this woman was caught in the very act of committing adultery' (8.4). There is a grim simplicity to the charge. She is hauled before Jesus with the smoking gun of her guilt written across her face, and plainly seen by those who have caught her, and the Law of Moses plainer still: she must be stoned.

Of course, the scribes and the Pharisees aren't really interested in catching this poor woman. It is Jesus they are after. And this question, 'Now what do you say?' (8.5), is just the means to catch him out. But like a bird escaping from the snare of the fowler, Jesus turns it back to them: 'Let anyone among you who is without sin be the first to throw a stone at her' (8.7). One by one they drop their stones to the ground and walk away.

Jesus demonstrates here an astonishing moral authority. He does not condone her sin. Far from it; he tells her to go away and sin no more. But he will not join in the blood lust of their swift judgement, gleefully pointing out the splinter in another's eye and wilfully ignoring the plank in their own. And to stand up to the crowd, to bear witness to a harder and more exacting ethic, is a beautiful sign of the new humanity that is born in Christ.

Eternal God,
give us insight
to discern your will for us,
to give up what harms us,
and to seek the perfection we are promised
in Jesus Christ our Lord.

COLLECT

Wednesday 6 March

Psalms **38** *or* **119.105-128**
Jeremiah 13.1-11
John 8.12-30

John 8.12-30

'I am the light of the world' (v.12)

It is with this amazing moral authority that Jesus now says that he is light. This is another astonishing claim. 'Let there be light' (Genesis 1.3) was the first word of God in creation, though we Christians understand Jesus to be not just created light for the world, but, with God in the beginning, the one through whom all things, including light, were made. As John himself puts it: 'All things came into being through him … and what has come into being through him was life, and the life was the light of all people. The light shines in the darkness, and the darkness did not overcome it' (John 1.3-5).

Now Jesus says that to follow him is to banish the darkness, to have the light of life. Therefore his judgement, as he had said to Nicodemus earlier, is that light has come into the world but people preferred darkness (see John 3.19).

Jesus then says: 'When you have lifted up the Son of Man, then you will realize that I am he' (v.28) – that is, the one sent from God to save, not condemn the world – 'and that I do nothing on my own … And the one who sent me is with me; he has not left me alone, for I always do what is pleasing to him' (vv.28–9). It is with these words, we are told, that many start believing in him again.

COLLECT

Almighty God,
whose most dear Son went not up to joy
    but first he suffered pain,
and entered not into glory before he was crucified:
mercifully grant that we, walking in the way of the cross,
may find it none other than the way of life and peace;
through Jesus Christ your Son our Lord,
who is alive and reigns with you,
in the unity of the Holy Spirit,
one God, now and for ever.

Psalms **56**, 57 *or* 90, **92**
Jeremiah 14
John 8.31-47

John 8.31-47

'… the truth will make you free' (v.32)

The truth that is revealed in Jesus will set you free. This is what Jesus says about his own message and his own ministry. It is what the Church teaches and proclaims. It is what we seek to embody as we travel through Lent and approach the great feast of Easter. But the people complain: 'We are descendants of Abraham and have never been slaves to anyone. What do you mean by saying, "You will be made free"?' (v.33).

Jesus is referring to a different sort of slavery: the slavery of sin. This is the slavery that stones adulterers, that so delights in the failings of others that it never sees its own shortcomings, that believes its justification with God is assured by birth and requires no penitence, no working out. Jesus even calls them children of the devil (v.44). What he means is that they are born of the one whose own self-deluding self-centeredness cut him off from the streams of grace and truth that were available and are now so readily available in the one who has come to forgive sins and to save the world. Jesus' forgiveness is free. But it is a gift that has to be accepted. You need to listen to what he is saying and what he is offering, and it is this they cannot do. Lent is also about our penitence. But whose voices are we listening to?

Eternal God,
give us insight
to discern your will for us,
to give up what harms us,
and to seek the perfection we are promised
in Jesus Christ our Lord.

COLLECT

27

Psalms **22** *or* **88** (95)
Jeremiah 15.10-end
John 8.48-end

John 8.48-end

'… before Abraham was, I am' (v.58)

Of all Jesus' words to his detractors, these are the most provocative. Throughout John's Gospel, Jesus begins many of his most famous sayings, by proclaiming 'I am'. I am the bread of life. I am the light of the world. I am the true vine. I am the way. I am the truth. I am the life. The words 'I am' are close to the very revelation of God's own name. 'I am who I am' says God to Moses. 'Tell the people, I am has sent you' (Exodus 3.14).

Jesus is therefore emphasizing his unity with the God who sent him, the God through whom, with him, the world was made. Abraham himself rejoices to see this day, the day the Christ of God comes into the world and reveals the purposes of God. 'Are you greater than our father Abraham, who died?' say the people (v.53). 'You are not yet fifty years old, and have you seen Abraham?' (v.57) I am before Abraham, replies Jesus. In fact, says Jesus, 'I am', meaning nothing less than I am God among you now.

This is when they reach for their stones again. This is either the most amazing truth or the most appalling blasphemy. They have reached their conclusion. This Jesus must die.

COLLECT

Almighty God,
whose most dear Son went not up to joy
    but first he suffered pain,
and entered not into glory before he was crucified:
mercifully grant that we, walking in the way of the cross,
may find it none other than the way of life and peace;
through Jesus Christ your Son our Lord,
who is alive and reigns with you,
in the unity of the Holy Spirit,
one God, now and for ever.

Psalms **31** *or* 96, **97**, 100
Jeremiah 16.10 – 17.4
John 9.1-17

John 9.1-17

'... eyes opened' (v. 10)

Up to this point we have had a number of long encounters with those who don't see and who don't hear. They just can't get who Jesus is. Now someone's eyes are opened. Jesus, who while he is in the world is the light of the world, encounters a man blind since birth. His disciples are worried about why the man is blind. Jesus is worried about how the man can be healed. The disciples want to know whose sins have caused the blindness. Jesus is determined that his blindness can be the means by which the works of God to bring light to all the world can be revealed. The blindness is not the result of sin. But it can be the means of grace. So he tells the blind man to wash himself in the pool of Siloam, and his sight is restored.

But some people even have trouble seeing that the man is healed. They think he must be someone else; and bringing him to the Pharisees all they can do is grumble that the healing has taken place on the Sabbath and is therefore proof, not of God's light coming into the world, but of Jesus' disregard for the ways of God. But others are troubled. It may be the Sabbath, but surely only someone from God could do such things? And now I wonder: can God do such things in me?

Eternal God,
give us insight
to discern your will for us,
to give up what harms us,
and to seek the perfection we are promised
in Jesus Christ our Lord.

COLLECT

29

Monday 11 March

Psalms 70, **77** *or* **98**, 99, 101
Jeremiah 17.5-18
John 9.18-end

John 9.18-end

'But now that you say, "We see", your sin remains' (v.41)

It is clear throughout this story that it is not just about a past physical healing but about our spiritual condition. The Pharisees reveal a lot about themselves when they ask 'Surely we are not blind?' (v.40). They have full confidence that their outlook on reality is trustworthy and in line with God's view of things. The Gospels teach us that Jesus did not so much answer people's questions as question their answers. He gently, but relentlessly, challenged people's belief in their first impressions – of themselves, others or God. The thing about first impressions is that they are not first. They come out of our past, influenced by our experiences of hurt and fear. *First Impressions* was going to be the title of the novel that Jane Austen eventually called *Pride and Prejudice*. Our initial reaction to people or situations can be distorted by our pride and our prejudices that we are so often unaware of. Consequently, our relationships can suffer.

Because first impressions are self-revealing, they also have the potential to be tools for self-revision. Jesus here tells the Pharisees that their sin is that they think they see properly. They are not open to transformation, to that new vision of absolutely everything that the lens of belief in God gives. Many think that sin is usually an innovation of some kind, but here it is surprisingly conservative, a desire to stay put in stale perceptions that are heavy with self-justification. It is very easy today to be seduced by quick clarity, the easy answer or the immediate defensive response. John shows us that Jesus subverts such poor judgement by his divine judgement – making the man, and all Christians with him – say in thankful amazement, 'he opened my eyes' (v.30).

COLLECT

Merciful Lord,
absolve your people from their offences,
that through your bountiful goodness
we may all be delivered from the chains of those sins
which by our frailty we have committed;
grant this, heavenly Father,
for Jesus Christ's sake, our blessed Lord and Saviour,
who is alive and reigns with you,
in the unity of the Holy Spirit,
one God, now and for ever.

Psalms 54, **79** *or* **106*** (or 103)
Jeremiah 18.1-12
John 10.1-10

John 10.1-10

'I came that they may have life, and have it abundantly' (v.10)

The image of Jesus as a gate has not captured the imagination as much as others have for some obvious, maybe artistic, reasons. However, in past centuries it would have been different. To Greek readers of this Gospel, Jesus referring to himself as a door would have resonated with their understanding, found in literature from Homer onwards, that a heaven above the earth was entered through such a gate. In the Jewish scriptures we also find many references to the heavenly gates such as in Psalm 118:

> 'Open to me the gates of righteousness,
> that I may enter through them
> and give thanks to the Lord.
> This is the gate of the Lord;
> the righteous shall enter through it.' (Psalm 118.19-20)

Many of us today feel as if we live on a threshold of faith, tentative about commitment because we are too full of questions or unease about what we may be getting ourselves into. In this passage, Jesus implies that, far from being a constricting route to a place where we have to surrender our integrity, to follow him means to 'come in and out and find pasture' (v.9). He opens up the way to a place of safety and rest, a sheepfold, where in all our confused hustle and bustle, it is the presence of the shepherd that reassures and makes life worthy of our trust. He has not come to close down the complexity of living but to enrich it and make it abundant.

COLLECT

Merciful Lord,
you know our struggle to serve you:
when sin spoils our lives
and overshadows our hearts,
come to our aid
and turn us back to you again;
through Jesus Christ our Lord.

Psalms 63, **90** or 110, **111**, 112
Jeremiah 18.13-end
John 10.11-21

John 10.11-21

'I am the good shepherd' (v.11)

What makes Jesus the 'good' shepherd? This passage makes the answer clear. He cares for his sheep in a way that a hired helper wouldn't understand. He knows, loves and protects his sheep and even lays down his life for them. Every Christian can pray the opening words of Psalm 23 with confidence: 'The Lord is my shepherd, I shall not want.'

Jesus also says here that his sheep know him (v.14). One of the things that people recognize as belonging to a shepherd is the shepherd's crook. Bishops carry one too as a sign of their pastoral vocation. Because of the curved end of the crook, it's usual to think that they are primarily used for reaching out and grabbing sheep around the neck, hauling them back in when being too independent or naughty. A Shropshire farmer once corrected this image for me. He said the crook was really for sticking deeply into the ground so that he could hold himself so still that the sheep eventually began to trust him.

This has many implications for bishops, and for all of us, as to what it is that establishes within us what is trustworthy and true. The rooted stillness of prayer and attention is where our compassion and responsibilities must all start. It is the same rootedness in the love of his Father (v.17) that draws us to Christ. His voice, with its words of life, is a part of that divine magnetism of mystery that brings peace to the human soul.

COLLECT

Merciful Lord,
absolve your people from their offences,
that through your bountiful goodness
we may all be delivered from the chains of those sins
which by our frailty we have committed;
grant this, heavenly Father,
for Jesus Christ's sake, our blessed Lord and Saviour,
who is alive and reigns with you,
in the unity of the Holy Spirit,
one God, now and for ever.

Psalms 53, **86** *or* 113, **115**
Jeremiah 19.1-13
John 10.22-end

John 10.22-end

'... he escaped from their hands' (v.39)

The French philosopher Voltaire once commented that 'God made man in his own image, and man returned the compliment'. It is true that we are all very skilled at making God a convenient reflection of ourselves. It is remarkable, too, how often God agrees with us and not with our opponents ...

The same is true with Jesus. Depending on who you talk to, he can be the conservative guardian of family life and traditional values or the radical subversive who attacks the establishment and the status quo. In this passage we find a heated conversation taking place as to who Jesus is: 'How long will you keep us in suspense?' (v.24).

In John's Gospel, we find that Jesus eludes our categories and definitions. Although much in the religious temperament can make us want to define and defend what it is we believe, the danger is that our soul forgets that it is always in school. The spiritual adventure to which we are called is a constant, often painful, journey in which our full-stops are changed into commas so that another chapter can begin in us and other lessons learned. Even at the end of John's Gospel, in the Easter garden, Mary Magdalene is asked not to cling to Jesus. She needs to be able to run if she is to become apostolic. The ancient Assyrians' word for prayer was the same as they had for the act of opening a clenched fist. We are not to be possessive of God for time will only teach us now, as in this passage's argument, that, 'he escaped from their hands' (v.39).

COLLECT

Merciful Lord,
you know our struggle to serve you:
when sin spoils our lives
and overshadows our hearts,
come to our aid
and turn us back to you again;
through Jesus Christ our Lord.

Friday 15 March

Psalms **102** *or* **139**
Jeremiah 19.14 – 20.6
John 11.1-16

John 11.1-16

'… he stayed two days longer in the place where he was' (v.6)

There is an irony at the heart of this passage. By returning to Judea to bring life, Jesus seals his own death at the hands of the authorities. The strange comment that Jesus decided not to go to Lazarus as soon as he heard Lazarus was ill (v.6) suggests that Jesus is in control of his destiny, choosing the times in which God is glorified and, at the same time, consciously offering his life to this end. The work of Jesus has its own hour, as the scholar Rudolf Bultmann put it.

As usual in John's Gospel, symbolic meaning is rich in almost every sentence. Jesus travels to give life to his friend to the ultimate cost of himself, and yet this story also suggests that what will happen in Bethany anticipates another resurrection, which will bring life to all he loves. 'This illness does not lead to death' (v.4) has a meaning as yet misunderstood by the disciples in the story, but may have been a comforting reassurance to those later disciples of the early Church suffering persecution and wondering to what end or purpose it was intended.

Thomas says that the disciples should follow Jesus, but we know that neither he nor the others yet knew what effect this would have on their lives. As Jesus starts out to go and raise Lazarus from the dead, the disciples eagerly in tow, a truth is outlined: God's gift to us is our being, and our gift to God is our becoming.

COLLECT

Merciful Lord,
absolve your people from their offences,
that through your bountiful goodness
we may all be delivered from the chains of those sins
which by our frailty we have committed;
grant this, heavenly Father,
for Jesus Christ's sake, our blessed Lord and Saviour,
who is alive and reigns with you,
in the unity of the Holy Spirit,
one God, now and for ever.

John 11.17-27

'I am the resurrection and the life' (v.25)

What does Jesus mean when he says that those who live and believe in him will never die (v.26)? One of the few things we know for certain is that one day our life will come to an end, so what is Jesus teaching? It becomes clear throughout this Gospel that life is defined as being in relationship with God. To be separated from the creator, the source of life and love, is deathly, and it is a separation that we perversely work on quite hard, not least by indifference and distraction. Even if we remain full of perplexed questions like Martha (v.21), the relationship with God that we forge in life has no end – nothing can possibly separate it, as St Paul taught (Romans 8.38-39). Yet, as in all relationships, it must be entered into with mutual freedom and expectancy.

When people today tell us to 'be realistic', what they tend to mean is that we should lower our expectations. For the Christian, to be realistic is the opposite. We fear God not because he is frightening or somehow out to get us, but because he is real and we are largely false or in hiding. It is his reality that exposes our artificiality and calls us out of darkness into a transforming relationship of light and life. Ultimately, our faith is not about our faithfulness towards God, but about his passionate fidelity to us, a fidelity we call resurrection and embodied in him we know as Christ.

Merciful Lord,
you know our struggle to serve you:
when sin spoils our lives
and overshadows our hearts,
come to our aid
and turn us back to you again;
through Jesus Christ our Lord.

COLLECT

Monday 18 March

Psalms **73**, 121 *or* 123, 124, 125, **126**
Jeremiah 21.1-10
John 11.28-44

John 11.28-44

'Jesus began to weep' (v.35)

The characters of Mary and Martha come to the fore in this passage. Martha, the frank-speaking one, has already gone out to meet Jesus to tell him that, if he had been with them, her brother wouldn't have died. Mary, though equally puzzled, reluctantly comes out and, weeping, kneels at his feet.

Together these women reveal the parts of bereavement that we will know something about – the questions and anger and frustration – and then the helplessness and submission to what has happened. When Jesus sees Mary crying, John says he did something. The English translation says that Jesus wept. John does not quite say this though. He says that Jesus shuddered with anguish; the Greek word implies a sort of snorting with fury, with flared nostrils, displaying an anger in his sadness. Perhaps it was an anger at the powers of sickness, death and human pain. If so, it reminds us in a Gospel that might sometimes appear to lead us another way, that Christ was fully human.

The seventeenth-century bishop Jeremy Taylor sometimes spoke of the 'gift of tears', an important challenge to the embarrassment we can often feel at our own or others'. Likewise, the poet John Donne prays that God will 'pour new seas into mine eyes' so that his world might be either drowned or washed. Jesus cried and, in doing so, blesses our tears and confusions and hurt. It may be part of the Christian vocation to help people cry better.

COLLECT

Most merciful God,
who by the death and resurrection of your Son Jesus Christ
delivered and saved the world:
grant that by faith in him who suffered on the cross
we may triumph in the power of his victory;
through Jesus Christ your Son our Lord,
who is alive and reigns with you,
in the unity of the Holy Spirit,
one God, now and for ever.

Psalms 25, 147.1-12
Isaiah 11.1-10
Matthew 13.54-end

Joseph of Nazareth

Matthew 13.54-58

'Is not this the carpenter's son?' (v.55)

The Church remembers St Joseph today, and this passage reminds us of the humble home and background that Jesus had – as well as the cynicism that can arise when someone comes back to their home town a changed person. People are obviously very taken with Jesus' teaching. 'Where then did this man get all this?', they ask (v.56).

We could answer this by pointing to the Gospel story so far, including an initiated ministry in the river Jordan, a distillation period in the desert and a day-by-day engagement with people in villages and towns, alongside his obvious study of the scriptures. All this has made Jesus the person he is. Matthew wants to say more though. Jesus has received his authority directly from God, and, just as Moses was chosen to speak words of life from the mountain only to find himself questioned on return, so Jesus in chapter 5 of Matthew's text preaches his beatitudes on the mount and now has his authority placed under similar scrutiny. To the jaundiced, everything begins to looks yellow, and Jesus, we are told, could not break the paralysis and the jeers of their disbelief.

Matthew has already told us (1.19) that Joseph was 'a righteous man' and unwilling to expose Mary to public disgrace. We feel something of his nature from this. He was the nurturer and encourager of Jesus as he grew up, the protector and teacher who provided security and wisdom. He may be simply referred to here as 'the carpenter' (v.55), but his love and faith in Jesus far outweigh the scepticism of his neighbours.

God our Father,
who from the family of your servant David
raised up Joseph the carpenter
to be the guardian of your incarnate Son
and husband of the Blessed Virgin Mary:
give us grace to follow him
in faithful obedience to your commands;
through Jesus Christ your Son our Lord,
who is alive and reigns with you,
in the unity of the Holy Spirit,
one God, now and for ever.

COLLECT

Wednesday 20 March

Psalms **55**, 124 *or* **119.153-end**
Jeremiah 22.20 – 23.8
John 12.1-11

John 12.1-11

'The house was filled with the fragrance' (v.3)

All four Gospels contain this story in various forms. Because of where John places it in his narrative, he suggests that Mary's act of love comes out of gratitude to Jesus for bringing her brother back to life. John also uniquely places this incident immediately before Jesus enters Jerusalem, where Jesus will be hailed as 'King of Israel' (vv.13,15), hinting that Mary's gesture is also an anointing before he takes his place on the throne of his cross.

The act of anointing Jesus' feet, when taken in its literary and cultural context, displays Mary's utter devotion to Jesus. The ointment she uses is precious and, since there is no indication that Mary belonged to one of the wealthier classes (the meal was served by Martha rather than a servant), the ointment was apparently a major expenditure. It is also significant that Mary wiped Jesus' feet with her hair, since well-kept hair contributed to a person's dignity in the ancient world. Women took pride in long hair, which was considered attractive, and damage to one's hair was considered degrading. In this act she heightens the sense of self-effacement already reflected in her willingness to serve him as a slave as she washes his feet.

Only Judas cannot see the intensity of the love that is being ritualized through such intimacy. Only Judas cannot smell the fragrance brought into the room. It is Mary who beautifully reflects the reckless generosity of God that day and not the pinched moralism of the betrayer.

COLLECT

Most merciful God,
who by the death and resurrection of your Son Jesus Christ
delivered and saved the world:
grant that by faith in him who suffered on the cross
we may triumph in the power of his victory;
through Jesus Christ your Son our Lord,
who is alive and reigns with you,
in the unity of the Holy Spirit,
one God, now and for ever.

Thursday 21 March

John 12.12-19

'His disciples did not understand these things at first' (v.16)

Jerusalem, though hailed as the city of God, had a bad reputation for being part of a domination system that encouraged political oppression and economic exploitation that was too often legitimized with religious language. Many prophets had tried to challenge the city with the justice of God, but now, as Jesus rides into the city, so a new reign begins. God's anointed breaks through into the heart of corruption and is greeted with hope and praise.

What the crowd does not yet understand is the cost to this regime-change where, in order to draw all people to himself (v.32), Christ is raised on a cross. Indeed, we are told that the disciples are a bit confused (v.16). They will soon learn more of the nature of Christ's vocation and the intensity of God's love for his people seen in his sacrifice. At the moment, they are happy to wave a branch with everyone else.

The community of Christian people known as the Church has been called a 'school for relating' in which, over time and through their prayer, each begins to learn how to relate more deeply to their self, to each other and to God. It requires patience and the ability to admit to the need for growth and some necessary un-learning. The Gospels are not afraid to tell us that the disciples were often baffled, squabbling and imperfect in their faith and faithfulness. It may be a new kingdom on earth that Christians work for, but this does not mean that they are not in need of constant revision themselves.

Gracious Father,
you gave up your Son
out of love for the world:
lead us to ponder the mysteries of his passion,
that we may know eternal peace
through the shedding of our Saviour's blood,
Jesus Christ our Lord.

COLLECT

39

Friday 22 March

Psalms **22**, 126 *or* 142, **144**
Jeremiah 24
John 12.20-36*a*

John 12.20-36*a*

'I, when I am lifted up from the earth,
will draw all people to myself' (v.32)

In today's passage, Jesus interprets his death and begins to reveal the cost of his kingship. He teaches that a grain dies in order to be fruitful, suggesting that his death will bring life to the world. This can seem as dark and impenetrable as the ground the seed is sown in. Jesus talks of how those who hate their life will keep it for eternal life. What does it mean to hate one's life? Is it to be able to deny one's own self for the sake of a greater good? Is it then a Christian truth that the human self is most itself when not being selfish? Certainly, teaches this Gospel, a Christian would be following their Lord if this truth were lived out: 'Whoever serves me must follow me' (v.26).

As Jesus talks in this passage, the Gospel becomes shadowed as Jesus' forthcoming death comes into focus. For whom will the sacrifice be made? When he preached in Pasadena in 2005, the Anglican archbishop Desmond Tutu gave the answer:

'When Jesus said, "I, when I am lifted up, will draw..." Did he say, "I will draw some"? "I will draw some, and tough luck for the others"? No. He said, "I, when I am lifted up, will draw all." All! All! All! – Black, white, yellow; rich, poor; clever, not so clever; beautiful, not so beautiful. All! All! It is radical. All! Saddam Hussein, Osama bin Laden, Bush – All! All! All are to be held in this incredible embrace. Gay, lesbian, so-called "straight". All! All! All are to be held in the incredible embrace of the love that won't let us go.'

COLLECT

Most merciful God,
who by the death and resurrection of your Son Jesus Christ
delivered and saved the world:
grant that by faith in him who suffered on the cross
we may triumph in the power of his victory;
through Jesus Christ your Son our Lord,
who is alive and reigns with you,
in the unity of the Holy Spirit,
one God, now and for ever.

John 12.36*b*-end

'After Jesus had said this, he departed and hid from them' (v.36)

I wonder whether it fits your image of Jesus to know that he hid from people? It is an extraordinary thought. Did he hide in a house? Alone? Behind a herd of animals? The reference to Jesus hiding comes immediately after him telling his disciples that while they have the light, they must believe in the light (v.36). John shows how little light is left, how it is going out, and becomes hidden. Indeed, it is here in the Gospel that the public ministry of Jesus comes to an end.

The New Testament scholar Raymond Brown divided John's Gospel into two unequal parts: the book of Signs (chapters 1 to 12) and the book of Glory (chapters 13 to 21). Here, at the end of the Signs book, Jesus recapitulates the topics, themes and motifs that have been presented so far. He tells his listeners that the word he has spoken 'will serve as judge' (v.48). Such judgement has a bad press. It is spoken of, and often painted, in terms of revenge, punishment and eternal pain. Judgement, however, is ultimately a liberating act for, at last, someone tells us the truth about ourselves and, though uncomfortable, we can begin to address our fault-lines, our past and our cruelties to others as well as to ourselves. Recognition is the first step to transformation, and to be shown our truth, in all its disturbing detail, frees us from our masks. Such truth sets us free, and Christ reassures us here that he did not come to judge the world in anger but to save it from itself with love.

COLLECT

Gracious Father,
you gave up your Son
out of love for the world:
lead us to ponder the mysteries of his passion,
that we may know eternal peace
through the shedding of our Saviour's blood,
Jesus Christ our Lord.

Monday 25 March
Monday of Holy Week

Psalm 41
Lamentations 1.1-12*a*
Luke 22.1-23

Lamentations 1.1-12*a*

'… any sorrow like my sorrow' (v.12)

On the Emmaus Road, the risen Jesus interprets the Scriptures to the two disciples (Luke 24.13-35). Jesus' question should be in our minds this Holy Week as we read the ancient familiar texts: 'Was it not necessary that the Messiah should suffer these things and then enter into his glory?' The events of Holy Week are foreshadowed and foretold in the Scriptures.

Lamentations is a series of five carefully constructed lyric poems that express the pain and grief of Jerusalem, personified in 1 and 2 as a grieving woman. Four of the poems are constructed around the different letters of the alphabet in the original Hebrew. The raw pain of the destruction of Jerusalem in 587 BC has been poured into verses written, most probably, for services on the site of the destroyed temple. We know of other similar laments from the ancient world in which a destroyed city grieves and waits for reconstruction.

The words give a shape to our suffering and provide a vocabulary for pain in every generation. But reading them at the start of Holy Week gives a particular focus. Six hundred years after the words were first sung, Jesus is crucified outside the same city. He takes to himself the sin and suffering and story of the City of David: 'Surely he has borne our infirmities and carried our diseases' (Isaiah 53.4). He takes to himself our own sin and suffering and story.

COLLECT

Almighty and everlasting God,
who in your tender love towards the human race
    sent your Son our Saviour Jesus Christ
to take upon him our flesh
and to suffer death upon the cross:
grant that we may follow the example of his patience and humility,
and also be made partakers of his resurrection;
through Jesus Christ your Son our Lord,
who is alive and reigns with you,
in the unity of the Holy Spirit,
one God, now and for ever.

Psalm 27
Lamentations 3.1-18
Luke 22.[24-38] 39-53

Lamentations 3.1-18

'... he shuts out my prayer' (v.8)

The voice changes. We move from the city personified as a woman to a song for every man in a deliberate balancing of genders (the Hebrew literally says 'I am a man who has seen affliction'). There are no references now to the destruction of a city. The verses speak of acute individual suffering in language familiar from the laments in the Psalms and in Job. The poetry is even more intense.

Most striking of all, echoing the Psalms, God is seen as the suffering man's adversary. It is God who is the subject of most of the verbs: God besieges, shuts out prayer, lies in wait, bends his bow and puts heavy chains on me.

When life brings terrible pain and it seems God is against us, the prayers of the Old Testament encourage us to express our anger and to make our complaint as we would in any deep relationship. Jesus stands in this tradition in the Garden of Gethsemane but especially on the cross. According to Mark and Matthew, Jesus cries out from the cross: 'My God why have you forsaken me?' quoting Psalm 22. It is not the end of the story, but the pain of separation from God is the deepest pain of all. Jesus has been to our darkest places and endured all we must endure.

True and humble king,
hailed by the crowd as Messiah:
grant us the faith to know you and love you,
that we may be found beside you
on the way of the cross,
which is the path of glory.

COLLECT

Wednesday 27 March

Wednesday of Holy Week

Psalm 102 [or 102.1-18]
Wisdom 1.16 – 2.1; 2.12–22
or Jeremiah 11.18-20
Luke 22.54-end

Jeremiah 11.18-20

'... like a gentle lamb led to the slaughter' (v.19)

Jesus is a prophet yet much more than a prophet. He stands in the long line of God's messengers who came not simply to deliver words but to bear witness in their lives to God's great love for his people.

The prophets' witness was often costly and involved pain, rejection, suffering and sometimes death. This is true of Jeremiah more than anyone. His ministry was in the generation leading up to the destruction of Jerusalem, and his word was one of judgement. His prophecy is punctuated by cries of lament and many tears for the suffering he endured.

This passage is one such lament. Jeremiah protests his innocence. The image of the gentle lamb led to the slaughter will be echoed in Isaiah 53.7 and again in all the language that describes Jesus as the Lamb of God. Jesus, too, is innocent of all charges against him and the victim of schemes and false accusation leading to his trial and his death.

Yet there is also a key difference between Jeremiah and Jesus. The prophet cries out, as we would do, for judgement and vengeance on his persecutors (v.20). The one who is more than a prophet is the one who prays even from the cross: 'Father, forgive them for they know not what they do' (Luke 23.34 AV).

COLLECT

Almighty and everlasting God,
who in your tender love towards the human race
    sent your Son our Saviour Jesus Christ
to take upon him our flesh
and to suffer death upon the cross:
grant that we may follow the example of his patience and humility,
and also be made partakers of his resurrection;
through Jesus Christ your Son our Lord,
who is alive and reigns with you,
in the unity of the Holy Spirit,
one God, now and for ever.

Psalms 42, 43
Leviticus 16.2-24
Luke 23.1-25

Leviticus 16.2-24

'… making atonement for himself and for the people' (v.24)

Jesus' death on the cross is such a great event it must be examined and explored from all sides. We have witnessed Jesus' identification with suffering and his fulfilment of the line of the prophets. Today, we see Jesus' fulfilment and completion of the Old Testament sacrificial system.

All communities and people have found ways of dealing with sin: the words, thoughts and actions that destroy lives and fellowship. This ancient text on the Day of Atonement describes the way of dealing with sin revealed in the Torah. On one day of the year, every year, one person, the high priest, offers a sacrifice of a bull and a goat and incense, and enters the sanctuary and the place of the mercy seat, the holy of holies. Over the head of a live goat this same high priest confesses the sins of the entire nation. The goat bears their iniquities into a barren region and is set free in the wilderness.

Jesus' death on the cross fulfils and completes the sacrificial system. There is no need for any further sacrifice. The curtain of the temple is torn in two at his death. The barriers between God and humanity are taken away. On this day we will remember that his body and blood are given 'for us' and 'for the forgiveness of sins'. We will remember that, in the words of the *Book of Common Prayer*, Jesus 'made there a full, perfect and sufficient sacrifice, oblation and satisfaction for the sins of the whole world'.

God our Father,
you have invited us to share in the supper
which your Son gave to his Church
to proclaim his death until he comes:
may he nourish us by his presence,
and unite us in his love;
who is alive and reigns with you,
in the unity of the Holy Spirit,
one God, now and for ever.

COLLECT

45

Friday 29 March

Good Friday

Genesis 22.1-18

'… your only son, whom you love' (v.2)

According to an ancient tradition, the bare hillside of Mount Moriah where Abraham climbed with his son Isaac was the site where Jerusalem would be built (2 Chronicles 3.1). Abraham is asked to offer his only son, whom he loves, in the very place where thousands of years later, the promises to Abraham would be fulfilled.

Abraham's son carries the wood for the offering as Jesus carries his cross on the first Good Friday. Isaac is then laid on the wood as Jesus submitted to the cross.

The story of God's command to Abraham is a terrible one. It takes us deep into Abraham's heart, where his love for his son and his faith in God are tested as iron is tested by fire.

Yet the story also gives us a lens through which we can watch the passion of Jesus Christ unfold today. It is the lens of a father's heart where the Father's love for his Son endures even as the Son suffers and gives his life for the sin of the world.

Abraham's faith shines through the story. He says to his servants: '*We* will come back to you' (v.5). He says to Isaac: 'God himself will provide the lamb for a burnt-offering' (v.8). This Good Friday, we are called to be children of Abraham, through the same faith that, through the death of Jesus on the cross, our sins are forgiven and we are accounted righteous before God.

COLLECT

Almighty Father,
look with mercy on this your family
for which our Lord Jesus Christ was content to be betrayed
    and given up into the hands of sinners
    and to suffer death upon the cross;
who is alive and glorified with you and the Holy Spirit,
one God, now and for ever.

Psalm 142
Hosea 6.1-6
John 2.18-22

Hosea 6.1-6

'… on the third day he will raise us up' (v.2)

The world will go about its business today. The shopping centres will be full. There will be football matches. There will be the bustle of the Bank Holiday weekend. Yet the Church throughout the world will wait and watch and pray.

We have travelled through this week on the way of the cross. The work of suffering is completed, but there is one great act of the drama still to come. And now there is this special Sabbath to look back on the last six days of the birth of a new creation and to strain forward on tiptoe to see what comes with tomorrow's dawn.

Hosea's words invite us in this very moment to a response: to return to the Lord, to come back once again to our first love, to find healing, a binding up of our wounds. We are invited to be raised up ourselves and to live before him.

Today is the day in between the first and third days: the day when Hosea's words will become a prophecy of resurrection fulfilled in Jesus, raised on the third day. And in his resurrection will be life and healing for all.

But today we wait and watch and pray and long for the showers, the spring rains to water the earth.

COLLECT

Grant, Lord,
that we who are baptized into the death
of your Son our Saviour Jesus Christ
may continually put to death our evil desires
and be buried with him;
and that through the grave and gate of death
we may pass to our joyful resurrection;
through his merits,
who died and was buried and rose again for us,
your Son Jesus Christ our Lord.

Seasonal Prayers of Thanksgiving

Passiontide

Blessed are you, Lord God of our salvation,
to you be praise and glory for ever.
As a man of sorrows and acquainted with grief
your only Son was lifted up
that he might draw the whole world to himself.
May we walk this day in the way of the cross
and always be ready to share its weight,
declaring your love for all the world.
Blessed be God, Father, Son and Holy Spirit.
Blessed be God for ever.

At Any Time

Blessed are you, creator of all,
to you be praise and glory for ever.
As your dawn renews the face of the earth
bringing light and life to all creation,
may we rejoice in this day you have made;
as we wake refreshed from the depths of sleep,
open our eyes to behold your presence
and strengthen our hands to do your will,
that the world may rejoice and give you praise.
Blessed be God, Father, Son and Holy Spirit.
Blessed be God for ever.

after Lancelot Andrewes (1626)

The Lord's Prayer and The Grace

Our Father in heaven,
hallowed be your name,
your kingdom come,
your will be done,
on earth as in heaven.
Give us today our daily bread.
Forgive us our sins
as we forgive those who sin against us.
Lead us not into temptation
but deliver us from evil.
For the kingdom, the power,
and the glory are yours
now and for ever.
Amen.

(or)

Our Father, who art in heaven,
hallowed be thy name;
thy kingdom come;
thy will be done;
on earth as it is in heaven.
Give us this day our daily bread.
And forgive us our trespasses,
as we forgive those who trespass against us.
And lead us not into temptation;
but deliver us from evil.
For thine is the kingdom,
the power and the glory,
for ever and ever.
Amen.

The grace of our Lord Jesus Christ,
and the love of God,
and the fellowship of the Holy Spirit,
be with us all evermore.
Amen.

Reflections for Daily Prayer
App

Make Bible study and reflection a part of your routine wherever you go with the Reflections for Daily Prayer App for iPhone, iPad and iPod Touch.

Download the app for free from the Apple App Store and receive a week's worth of reflections free. Then purchase a monthly, three-monthly or annual subscription to receive up-to-date content.

Use your iPhone QR code reader to scan this symbol and visit the Reflections for Daily Prayer page at the App store.

Orders can be made at **www.chpublishing.co.uk** or via **Norwich Books and Music** Telephone **(01603) 785923** E-mail **orders@norwichbooksandmusic.co.uk**

Resources for Daily Prayer

Common Worship: Daily Prayer

The official daily office of the Church of England, *Common Worship: Daily Prayer* is a rich collection of devotional material that will enable those wanting to enrich their quiet times to develop a regular pattern of prayer.

It includes:

- Prayer During the Day
- Forms of Penitence
- Morning and Evening Prayer
- Night Prayer (Compline)
- Collects and Refrains
- Canticles
- Complete Psalter